GOD MADE ME PERFECT AND WONDERFUL

A Daily Devotional for Children

Icilda V. Hogan

Written by
Icilda V. Hogan

Pictures by
Victor V. Hogan II

AuthorHouse™
1663 Liberty Drive, Suite 200
Bloomington, IN 47403
www.authorhouse.com
Phone: 1-800-839-8640

First published by AuthorHouse   3/24/2009

ISBN: 978-1-4389-2665-0 (sc)

Printed in the United States of America
Bloomington, Indiana

This book is printed on acid-free paper.

authorHOUSE®

All scriptures reference is paraphrased from the New King James, NIV and the Amplified versions of the Bible. Paraphrasing the scriptures makes it easier for children to understand and apply them to their lives.

Published in the United States of America in 2008
Text © copyright 1999 by Author, Icilda V. Hogan
Photograph-illustration © copyright 2003 by Victor V. Hogan II

DEDICATION

I dedicate this book to my 8 grandchildren, Christian, Caelan, Maya, Zachary, Langston, Gabriel, Ella and Naomi, who God made perfect and wonderful.

ACKNOWLEDGEMENT

Thanks to my husband, Victor I; my daughter, Vanessa; my daughter-in-law, Ahsa; and my cousin, Darcy for their encouragement and prayers. Special thanks to the illustrator, Victor II, who is my gifted son. Above all, thanks to my Heavenly Father who chose me to write this book to encourage children to establish a time of communion with Him.

Dear Parents:

GOD MADE ME PERFECT AND WONDERFUL is designed to help your children establish a daily devotional time with God. If they are not able to read yet, have them repeat the confessions after you. This book will also teach them to recognize the different parts of their body as well as how to spell them.

Please take the opportunity to lead your children to Christ by having them repeat the following prayer of salvation.

PRAYER OF SALVATION

God, I believe that Jesus is Your Son.

I believe that He died for my sin.

Jesus, please come into my heart and save me.

Thank you Jesus for saving me.

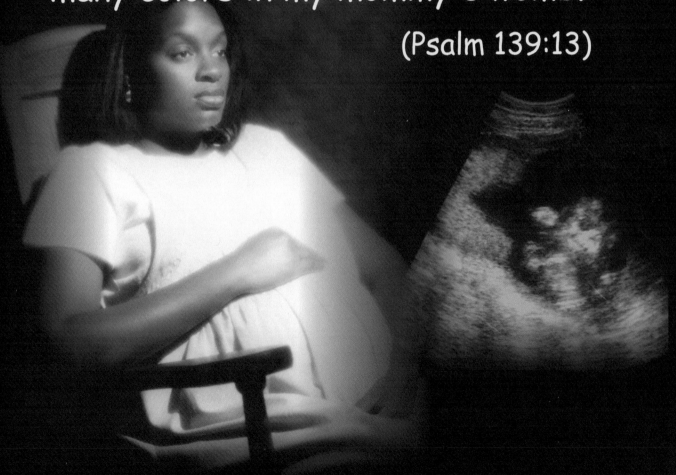

God, You made my whole body. You made my inside parts and You made my outside parts. You knit me with many colors in my mommy's womb.

(Psalm 139:13)

God, thank You for making my head, with my MIND, perfect and wonderful.

I have a sound, calm and peaceful MIND.   (II Timothy 1:7)

MIND

God, thank You for making my EYES
perfect and wonderful.

EYES

Blessed and happy are my EYES because they do see.

(Matthew 13:16)

God, thank You for making my EARS perfect and wonderful.

God, open my EARS, and I will hear and listen to what You are saying. (Isaiah 50:4)

God, thank You for making my NOSE perfect and wonderful.

God, I can breathe so I will praise You.

(Psalm 150:6)

NOSE

God, thank You for making my LIPS perfect and wonderful.

My LIPS will shout for joy when I sing praises to You. (Psalm 71:23)

LIPS

God, thank You for making my TONGUE perfect and wonderful.

TONGUE

My TONGUE will talk of Your righteous acts all day long.

(Psalm 71:24)

God, thank You for making my MOUTH perfect and wonderful.

My MOUTH shall be filled with Your praise, Your glory and Your beauty all day long.   (Psalm 71:8)

MOUTH

God, thank You for making my NECK perfect and wonderful.

God, help me to wear your Word around my NECK as a pretty necklace, so when I walk I will not stumble and fall. And when I lay me down to sleep, I will not be afraid and my sleep will be sweet.

(Proverbs 3:22-24)

God, thank You for making my

HANDS perfect and wonderful.

God, please take me by my right HAND and show me what You want me to do

(Psalm 73:-23-24)

HAND

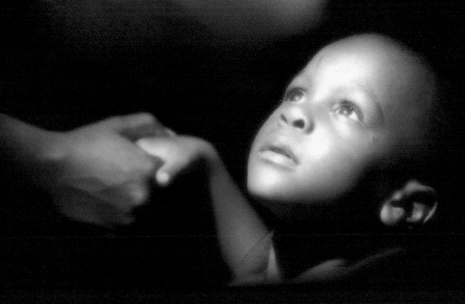

God, thank You for making all of my organs, especially my HEART,

perfect and wonderful.

God, please give me a clean HEART that I would know what is good and what is bad.   (I King 3:9)

HEART

God, thank You for making my LEGS perfect and wonderful.

God, I will praise You with a dance.
(Psalm 149:3)

LEGS

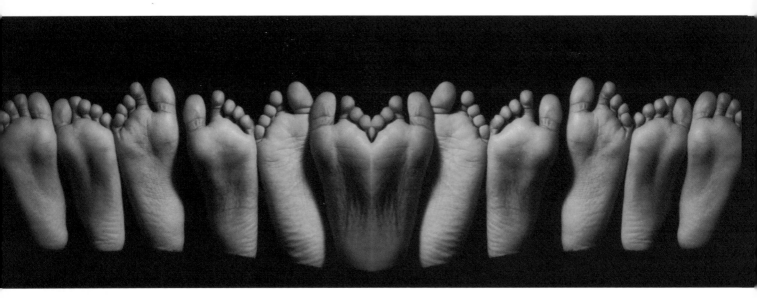

God, thank You for making my FEET
perfect and wonderful.

God, please direct and guide my FEET that I may walk in peace.

(Luke 1;79)

FEET

Printed in the United States
142990LV00001B